I0438007

DON'T CATCH THE RECESSION DEPRESSION

Written and Felt by Victor Zapata

authorHOUSE®

AuthorHouse™
1663 Liberty Drive, Suite 200
Bloomington, IN 47403
www.authorhouse.com
Phone: 1-800-839-8640

First published by AuthorHouse 4/1/2009

ISBN: 978-1-4389-6516-1 (sc)

Printed in the United States of America
Bloomington, Indiana

This book is printed on acid-free paper.

I want to dedicate this book to my better half my soul mate Dawn, and to my little princess Deevyne. Most of all I want to dedicate this book to all the Americans that are going through tuff times right now as we speak. I want you to know that there is hope and no matter how bad things get. Or how dark it is as we walk this unpredictable tunnel we call life .There will always be light at the end of it!

This book is not intended to only reach those who are unemployed, of any certain race or specific religion, financial status or anyone in particular. My intentions and hopes are that as many house holds across America as possible can receive the message I am trying to send here. Which is if we don't take a part and participate in changing our country, we will first hand witness everything we believe in and are accustomed to fall to the ground.

Contents

An act of kindness

What can we do when are best harvest goes bad? Due to natural or malicious acts?

Are we to just give up? Waive a white flag and say we have had enough? And never

Plant a harvest again?

What are we to do when those appointed to high ranking positions, elected officials or educated individuals commit foolish acts and lie to us and deceive us?

By speaking untrue facts and rubbish and not telling us what we need to hear but what we want to hear.

- Do we give up on democracy and turn into a dictator ship or even communism?
- Do we quit school or become ignorant and commit foolish acts?

All because of a handle full of individuals who lack integrity and morals are deluded?

Of course not, we were meant for better and greater things, our minds were meant to soar as a crowd we shall uproar!

My name is unimportant

- My credentials,
- Educational background
- Religious beliefs
- Ethnical background
- Financial and social status in society irrelevant

All that matters is that my message gets across to you if you give me the chance to plant the seed of knowledge in your mind, you will find

That only then will we be able to prevent the things we can control, look hard into our soul, turn to our neighbor in need and honestly and willingly their pain and hearts console.....

It is up to you and me to keep this the home of the brave and the land of the free!

Insight

Throughout this book that you're about to read, you will get an insight on different scenarios that take place in many households across America. Hopefully my book opens your eyes to the terrible things that take place behind close doors. Some of these scenarios you might not be able to relate to. But I strongly believe you need to know about. While you read my book maintain an open mind on how others feel with their situations that they might be facing.

HOW TO AVOID THE RECESSION DEPRESSION.....

Hello America if you're reading this book it's because it probably caught your eye due to the fact that you're also unemployed like I was. Maybe it's an ex coworker, a cousin, an old friend, a significant other. By picking up this book for yourself or someone else you made a good choice. Taking the time to read this book will not only lift your spirits, bring back the hope we have lost, hopefully it changes your life like writing changed mine. Most of all let you know that there is light at the end of the tunnel we have entered some purposely, some unknowingly.

This economy is affecting every one there is no one that is immune to this disease that has infected our great country and brought it too its knees. Yes the unthinkable has happened. What will our next move be? Are we going to waive the white flag and call it quits? Of course not this country was and still is a country that was made by strong minded and strong willed individuals that gave up their lives so we might see better tomorrow's Granting us the right to say what we want, read what we want, and pray to whom we want. "Was that all done in vain"? Certainly not!! I am sure with out a reasonable doubt that we will pull out of this economical crisis we have fallen into and has shattered us into pieces. Since the great day in history that we were named the United States of America to this day our name has not changed and forever will be the same. Signifying that we are united and that way we shall stay! Are we not the same country that fought several countless wars and came out triumphant when others said it couldn't be done? Did we not already survive one recession in the past already? Did we not contribute most of the greatest technological break through known to man? Weren't we the first country to send a man to the moon? If we can accomplish these great things there is nothing out of our reach and nothing impossible!

That is why we cannot lose hope in our great country which has gave us several privileges and entitlements that others would have not .We have to basically restore the damages our country has gone through. Now you might be asking yourself where I begin. Very simple lets start off by being more conservative in our spending minimize our wants from our needs. I'm not talking about keeping all your money under your mattress or in a sock at home inside your favorite coat pocket. I'm talking about do some research on your bank. See if they are going through economical problems if they are what assure you that your money is safe with them, and ask for their facts not that "I want you to stay with us, or open a new account with us" mumble jumbo!

The truth is if we don't keep the money flowing into the economy we are not going to see no changes. All the big corporations are making adjustments to deal with this economical crisis that we are in, resulting in thousands of people getting laid off on a daily basis. If they are coping with it why cant we? Easier said than done it's a proven fact the majority of Americans where riding the credit, bad mortgage, and bad loans train never thinking it might crash. Well it did and now we are all paying for it in one way or another. Some get laid off, others take salary cuts, and others have to take on more responsibilities due to the fact that they can't afford an extra hand no more.

If you are currently working my advice to you is, if you don't have a savings account yet open one. Start putting money into it whatever you can, however you can don't wait till it's too late and you get that pink or yellow or whatever color your lay off paper maybe to do it. Be on time if you're not pulling your weight at the job this is the perfect time to start. Try not to miss unless really necessary, don't give the corporation monster a reason to lay you off.

As for the all of you that are currently unemployed my heart goes out to you it really does I know what it's like trust me. I've dealt with the half hour E.D.D phone calls, that only let you speak to an automated service that doesn't even care about you. Can hardly understand you and just drives you nuts and only makes you more frustrated than you already are.

I know how frustrating it can be to drive around looking for work all day filling out as many applications as you can, trying to conserve as much gas as you possibly can.

WHY ARE PEOPLE HERE IN THIS COUNTRY? OR EVEN COME TO SETTLE IN THIS COUNTRY?

People have come to this country over the past centuries not only for their great land marks, or great weather? Because they weren't always there yes that might be part of the reason. But the main reason is that this country is known as the land of great opportunity! You here stories about immigrants that have came poor to this country and have built successful businesses and made great contributions to our every day life. The Asian community has given us Chinese food, and a lot of the technology we have and use on a daily basis. China, India, Thailand, Indonesia, and Japan play a huge role in the shipping and making of hundreds, of our materials that are manufactured over seas. The Italian culture bring us there delicious pastas and of course pizza and other fine dishes and deserts, and contributions they have made. The African American culture and people like Martin Luther king have made huge contributions.

Such things as the street lights and fought for equal rights in not only the African American community but for all minorities in the community as well. The Latino people and cultures have given us great food such as tacos, enchiladas, and other great dishes. Given our nation many imported and exported good to eat and use in our grocery stores. Latino people like Caesar Chavez also fought for those who no one would fight for, and given us a better look at how important it is to treat every worker equal. No matter how big or small his or her job maybe. The English, polish, German, Jewish, Puerto Rican, Native Americans and other cultures that have settled here or were settled here and have called this great country home. Have changed the way we live and function on a daily basis. I just want to give them credit and all those I didn't mention also. Whether it be in the kitchen, a medical room, laboratory , tire shop, your phone provider, a simple movie on the big screen, a lab class, in a warehouse, or in a sea dock all the contributions made by every one are need and would affect us drastically if one of them have not been made.

If our economy does not change, a lot of these people that have come to this country will be forced to leave and close there shops down forever. Return to there home land that might be stricken with poverty or incurable disease's or even lack of a good educational system.

The special someone scenario.....

Coming home frustrated because you still can't find work anywhere and the bills are just building up more and more and you run out of extensions on your utilities. Your car is about to get repossessed so your thinking about hiding it at some ones house. Then you notice that most of your neighbor's homes are up for foreclosure and they might not be there tomorrow. You have ran out of options and your car winds up getting taken and now your stuck looking for work on the bus, and your kids have to walk to school.

You feel worse now, more than you did before and your better half isn't talking to you anymore. Him or her which ever opposite sex you have keeps telling you what kind of provider are you? Is it really that hard to get a job? Why haven't you got a job yet? The bills are due what are we going to do about food? We already lost our car what else is it going to take to open your eyes?

Arguing every day you guys don't even sleep together anymore. You feel bad for your children because they have to watch the whole thing and when they ask you if you guys are going to separate? You lie and say that you just need mommy, and daddy time. Your kids ask you for money to buy something on the way home and it just break's your heart because you just manage to pay your rent with your unemployment check.

Then the unexpected happens when you get that letter stating that the government has ran out of funds their cutting your unemployment and at the end it states they wish you the best of luck in your journey! You crumble it in your hand; furious, your eyes are getting watery filled with tears. You wish you could just swallow this letter and pretend it never came. How are you going to explain this to your significant other? There is no sugar coating this it's a harsh reality like it or not. First to go is your pride, and then your dignity, and your apartment or home follows.

Leaving you and your loved ones in a tiny hotel room because that's all you can afford. Applying for aid is a nightmare the room is packed you got to pull a number and it takes forever to be seen .Yet you're thankful to at least have that as a resort. You've already pawned most of your jewelry, and other items you know you might never see again.

Your still on the hunt for a job you get more and more stressed out every day that goes by it seems like the more you try the fewer results you get. You keep telling yourself tomorrow things will be different but when tomorrow comes the results are the same. You're still unemployed and you're still on bad terms with your better half. Child care is threatening to cut you if you don't find a job within their time frame (which is thirty days). Sending you form after form, setting up appointment after appointment they don't want to hear it. The whole process is driving you mad you're just sick and tired of it all. There response to you is that there are too many people that need our services and we just can't focus on your case. This is some of the feedback answers you get from these workers that are assigned to your case. A choice must be made quickly. Day thirty has come and you haven't found a job yet. The answer is easy to see you and your significant other have to break up so your kids can stay in childcare.

There are no If's and Buts' about it you've official became another weekend parent, and this economy just cost you your home, your family and you significant other. Time keeps on moving on and it doesn't wait for no one either you jump aboard or get left behind. Now your stuck in a cross road not knowing which way to go next?

If you are single and feel lost about not having no one there for you imagine what this individual must be feeling like dealing with these hard times with an obnoxious or uncompassionate other? The truth is some things are harder to deal with when you got more than one mouth to feed.

Dealing with the Unemployment Madness and Falling Victim to the Recession Depression Alone....

Coming home to your small apartment after a long days work trying to get dressed as quickly as possible because you have to jump in the shower and get ready to go to your second job in a half hour. I literally meaning you have to jump in and out as quick as you can and scrum up some kind of lunch, or you're just going to starve all night like you did the last two nights. You try no to do that because you know it will eventually take a toll on you running on low sleep and hardly any food you're off to work again.

This was suppose to be just for a short period of time, but it feels like a life time now, and it's finally taking a toll on you. The bags under you eyes are becoming more and more noticeable each and everyday that goes by. Talking less at work because the lack of sleep is catching up to you and you don't want anyone to notice it. Eating your lunch as quick as possible just so you can go to the back of the building or even to your car and take a thirty minute cat nap which isn't going to do much for you "but god knows how good it feels to be a sleep". You haven't been waking up on time from your little cat naps and they have already given you verbal and written warnings due to these irresponsible cat naps. The images of those write ups, and verbal warnings given and said to you cross your mind as you lie down and go to sleep.

You wake up and you realize your shift is over! Oh my god you say to yourself as you run out of your car not even fixing your hair, marks on your forehead from your dash board still imprinted on you face. Now running up and down the job floors, like a crazy person. Looking for your boss hoping to explain what had happened to you before it was too late. You tell yourself hopefully he didn't notice but the truth is the chances of that happing are very low. You finally find him and try to explain but its too late he tells you "people are complaining about you, that they have to perform more work duties because you don't make it back on time I got to let you go I'm truly sorry" he tells me. With disappointment in his voice he tells me "pick up your last check tomorrow". You feel like your life is over, you know that without this job you will really not be able to afford your little apartment.

The next day is like a big blur, you try not to think about it. Fighting the urge not to panic, knowing that if you panic you will probably get an anxiety attack. You know in your mind no Inhaler, or even blowing air into a little brown paper bag will make you feel better you can try it till your blue in the face. Your anxiety level is now high breathing deeply, and sweating in an uncontrollable manner nothing seems to calm you down. You hate it when you're confronted with these kinds of problems that you have to face and can't avoid. You jump on the phone and try to apply for unemployment but your signal keep's fading. There's really nothing you can do since you're on a cell phone, and can't afford a house phone. Basically you just wasted another half hour, of you're anytime minutes, which you really don't have and will wind up paying an easy two hundred dollar on your next phone bill. Being realistic you don't even have two hundred dollars to pay it and it will wind up in collection. Granting them the permission to harass you all day long, and are able to send you countless letters until you pay them. All because the automated service just told you that," Due to the number of volume of calls that they are receiving, your call cannot be answered at this moment please hang up and try again later".

The following day you go down to the unemployment office only to see that it's jammed packed. You wait in the lobby for some one to get off the computer so you can get on cal jobs and look for a job. Browsing through all the categories you try applying for every opening available, even fast food. That's when you come to realize all these people at the unemployment office are here for the same reason. They are probably applying for the same exact jobs you're applying for and it discourages you. While waiting for your phone interview you've discovered that two weeks have goes by before finally getting your phone interview. Hoping its good news, they tell you we're sorry but we're going to have to deny you unemployment due to some penal code you can't even understand.

At least you still have you other job you tell yourself as you walk in from your lunch. Seconds later your boss hands you a pink slip and a box of sees candies. Saying they really appreciate everything you have done for the company and to not hesitate to use her or him as a reference and to keep in touch. The rent is due in a few days. There is no food in the fridge and you don't know which way to turn. You're balled up in the corner of your now almost empty apartment. Wishing you could just erase yourself off the face of the earth, but reality is you can't! Your in a cross road and you don't know which way to go next?

If you have some one by your side now that is helping you cope with these hard times, Regardless if they are perfect or not at least you got some one by your side. Imagine what this individual must be feeling like dealing with all these hard times alone.

WHEN ITS NOT YOU THAT'S UNEMPLOYED? DOES IT STILL AFFECT ME?

INSIDE THE HOME

Your parents are fighting and you just don't know why? They tell you everything is okay. But for some weird reason you know that they are not being completely honest with you. You ask them for a happy meal and they say they can't buy it for you right now maybe tomorrow. They've been saying that for about two weeks now. You notice they hardly even talk at the table while eating dinner. You ask your parents why we can't eat something other than the same old things we eat on a daily basis. They just yell at you and tell you to be thankful that you're eating something. You notice that they have been yelling at you more and more everyday. Things are just not the same no more your parents just push you to the side. Late at night you just close your eyes and pray things get better with your family. When your parents weren't arguing as much as they do now, your dad had a job and he wasn't gone all day looking for work .Only to come home frustrated and angry with no time to spend with you. You say amen, jump into bed and hope tomorrow will better.

The next day is no better than the day before. You wake up to loud cursing and screaming done by your parents. Mommy's slamming doors and saying where are we going to go? Daddy's sitting on the couch slouched down with a three day notice letter in his had rocking back and forth like a mad man He gets up and storms out of the house yelling that it wasn't his fault while ripping the letter in two ! I asked what the matter was and Mommy says were not going to school today that we got to go apply for welfare. What's welfare? I asked? Your mommy answers "It's when your mommy and daddy don't have money to pay the rent" and they need a place to live. Still confused I followed my mommy into the car quietly and quickly. Thinking to myself are we going to be without a home?

The welfare must be really busy like Santa is during Christmas time! Because when we got there, there were plenty of kids to play with. It was very full and there were some people that smelled really bad. My mommy just kept telling me to not stare at them or make fun of them. I decided to sit down and watch the movie that they were playing while we waited. After hours of waiting, we finally got seen by some lady that couldn't even remember my mommy's name. She was asking my mom all kinds of questions. I was starting to think they were going to take my mommy to jail so

I hugged her tightly. Finally we left when my mommy got a plastic card and a check. Where are we going to go now mommy, I'm tired I want to take a nap in my bed"? I asked, she replied with anger in her voice "you ask too many questions just get your seatbelt on". I took it she was mad so I didn't say a word the rest of the time we drove.

We pulled up to a hotel it was really scary. I hated living there we where all cramped up in one room. I just want to go back home, I was too scared to ask my parents if we were going to stay here permanently because I knew they would yell at me. I just wanted my family to be happy again. I didn't want to be ignored anymore, I wanted my daddy to chase me around the house like he use to. I wanted my mommy to make her famous doughnuts with cinnamon and sugar again. The only time I got to play was at school I was at a cross road now not knowing which way to go?

We never take the time to realize that what we are going through is also affecting our children. ! Well it is! More and more kid's homes are being broken everyday due to the economy. We as parents must stop and realize that we cannot keep pushing our kids to the side or neglect them especially in this time of need. What most parents don't realize or think of is that our body language and actions says a whole lot. Our kids pick up on it, and may even mock us and act out, in a rebellious kind of way at school. Things may escalate from the lack of discipline and interest in school to get as serious as yelling and hitting other kids. So please lets be more self conscious about the language and things we do in front of our little ones. My advice to you is that if you are dealing with problems at home and you do have kids. No matter what there ages may be don't speak about your financial problems in front of them. Don't lie to them neither just tell them that you guys just have to watch what you buy a little more. Making sure you keep everything behind close doors.

Take them to the museums most of them are free and only ask for a small donation it s a cheap way to have fun, and I'm sure that the kids will love it. Take them to the park let them air out play with them and show them that you love them.

THE HARD WORKER TAKEN FOR GRANTED, WORKING AGAINST HIS WILL DURING THE RECESSION .....

Another long day at work thank god it's over! Everyday seems to get longer and longer. The job I once had a passion for, and I use to look forward to everyday has now became a burden on me. I remember when I got my first pay check and opened it and the amount said one thousand dollars and it had my name on it I was so happy. I thought I had finally made it. Thinking I had made my first decent amount of money in my whole life. Sadly, as the days and months went by, I lost all interest in the job I once loved. I continued to work countless hours in overtime and was unable to get any days off. I began to notice that I wasn't being paid all my hours including my overtime pay. The amount of hours on my time card didn't match up to what my paycheck said. Regardless if you got paid or not you were expected to get to work on time, and work as many hours as they expected of you. Holidays without a doubt were being worked as well.

I would work months at a time without a single day off .They weren't eight hour days, neither I'm talking about straight up twelve hour shifts. These guys would work you till your hair fell out and you dropped to the ground from exhaustion! All that mattered to these people was production and to make there quota at the end of the month. They did whatever it took to get things done as quickly as possible using the cheapest of materials and labor. Honestly it seemed like everyday they were thinking of knew ways to increase production and cut back on costs, which I know is some thing smart to do. But why make your worker's struggle more and waste more time due to cheap materials and run down equipment. These people would run the machines to the ground, go days without doing any kind of maintenance to their machines. So it was no surprise that the equipment was always breaking down on us.

I seen plenty of people come and go while I worked there. They all talked a good one that they could keep up with the over time and that it wouldn't affect them. Slowly but surely they would all end up quitting. There were some people that would actually quit on there first day. They would not even make it past the first eight hours. Before they would be running out the door and going to the human resources dept to resign. There was a lot of people getting hired and fired at this company. It seemed like for every one person that got fired there was someone else getting hired. They had a pretty good system worked out I guess. It even seemed like they were throwing job fairs every month.

I worked in the production dept which was where all the action happened especially on my machine we were the highest in demand out of all the other machines it was nothing nice I worked with chemicals and fiber glass. I remember my first day working there people would ask me where do you work? Not aware that I was in the work area with the worst working conditions. I would respond to them I work on the fiber machine and they would just stay looking at me with there mouths wide open in astonishment. Everyone knew it was nothing nice to work there. Some people quit due to the fiber glass that would cause you to scratch the hell out of your skin. Others would quit because of all the chemicals and all the fumes that you would inhale working there. Whatever the reason most people who started there would not make it there even a month.

I have been working here a whole three years and I was way over my head in debt with my bills. I felt like no matter how much over time I would work. My check would never be enough to cover the rent and all of our bills. I had just had a newborn baby and I had three other kids of my own and things weren't easy on me and my wife. My wife and I would argue all the time because I was never home. I was always at work and couldn't go anywhere with her. I was unable to go to any of the parties, Family functions she was invited to. I was always tired! If I went somewhere I was always falling asleep everywhere this caused us to argue. This job had cost me many nights filled with lack of sleep and arguments, and now it was about to cost me my family.

What gets me mad the most? Is that I know that I can't lose this job I got too much riding on this job this is my families only source of income. What's going to happen to my family if I lose this job or get laid off? I have been watching the news theirs a lot of employers that are going to lay off a lot of workers due to the economy. What should I do? Should I quit my job? Keep putting up with all this nonsense I'm going through? Getting changed out in that filthy locker room into my blue uniform made me think. I know I'm stuck in a crossroad and I need to figure out how to get myself out of this mess I placed myself in.

If you have never worked a job that has forced you to work against your own will you might not know what this individual is going through. I know what you're saying, isn't that against the law? Your right! But when Wall Street is going under, and the job market is dropping to the ground. You can't afford to lose your job and leave your kids at home to starve. Look at things from this perspective? Is it going to be you're civil rights? Or your own flesh and blood starving and becoming homeless? The outcome wouldn't have been pretty if you wanted to be the hero in this company. I'm not saying that it is right what took place in this scenario. All I'm saying is that these types of things do happen.

THE STAY HOME MOM WITH THE RECESSION DEPRESSION

I'm so stressed out they cut Vincent's hours this week. Unlike every other night tonight he came home more upset than on most nights. He stormed straight into the kitchen and said "Can you believe that there is talk about a huge lay off in my department honestly after all the hours I gave these guys they better not lay me off". What do you think? Do you think they will lay me off honey? I didn't know how to respond to him so I just stood quite and continued to cut the onions I needed. Since I didn't respond to him he just slammed the fridge door grabbed a beer and headed for the garage. I could tell he was very angry. What was I suppose to say? I don't know what to say to him anymore. Whatever comes out of my mouth is wrong and is just going to cause argument. Besides I have my own problems to deal with. He's having problems at work, and I m having problems at home. I don't think I can handle this much stress in my life all by myself. If I wanted to be single I would have never gotten married to begin with. I'm trying to be the best wife I could possibly be. I've even cut back on unnecessary spending, eating out included. It's hard trying to hide the way I feel in front of the children. Inside I' m worried sick, but on the outside I'm pretending like I'm happy for the kids. I don't think I can continue on with this masquerade any longer it's taking a toll on me and I don't feel right lying to the kids. Late at night I sit up in my room and cry after I put the kids to bed. I know I have to be stronger but I can't do this alone .Vincent is becoming more distant and doesn't want to talk about it .When I bring it up he just tells me to be quite and to leave him alone.

I think I'm going to have a nervous breakdown, I don't have anyone to talk to and things are only getting worst. I need to know that everything is going to be okay and that my family and I are going to get through these hard times. To be honest with you its hard sometimes all the stress does get to me. Oftentimes, I find myself taking it out on my kids and my husband. Sometimes I feel like I'm the one that's going to get laid off. The way I look at things is that there not only going to lay off my husband they're going to lay off my whole family. If he loses his job we will have no food in the fridge or money to pay our bills. I have tried to get a job but who's going to watch my kids for me while I work? I have four kids and I'm the only one that has looked after them since they were babies. So what do I do now? I really feel like just throwing in the towel and calling it quits. With me always being a stay at home mom I never took education seriously. So now I think to myself who will really hire me with no up to date skills.

Now let me give you a little insight on how my husband and I use to be before the economy came crashing down. My husband and I were always happy we would take the kids out and we would go eat dinner at our favorite restaurants .We would go camping, the beach or we would just jump in the car with all the kids and go watch a movie as a family. I use to make dinner every night and if the kids were good I would give them some of there favorite ice cream or a snack. I paid all the bills on time and the rent was never late. We never had a late fee to pay, we even had cable we would rent movies on demand.

Once the economy started tumbling down, all that went out the window. We cut back on the road trips because the high gas prices; along with the dinner trips they were putting a hole in our pockets. We cut back on our family activities and I had to manage our money better. I started to buy cheaper things at the super market just so our money would go to what was needed and not what we wanted. My husband and I adapted to the change quicker than the kids. They are still having a hard time getting use to the change. It's hard on them they were use to getting rewarded for being good at school and getting good grades on their report cards. The truth is ever since the economy has gotten bad and my husband's hours have gotten shorted. It's been a long time since the children have seen any kind of rewards. I honestly think thins are not going to get better just yet, it's going to be a long time before things go back to the way they use to be in my house.

I just wish my husband would just get out of the being in the denial stage he is in and just talk to me. We would be able to get through these hard times better, if we stuck together and we didn't fight as much as we do. I'm stuck in a cross road and I just don't know what to do, or which way to go?

Us as providers get so caught up in the putting food on the table cycle and have been playing that role for so long. That we forget what was the sole purpose of us taking that responsibility on to begin with. As sad as it may sound we actually forget that there's people that sit on the table we work so hard to keep food. What I mean by that is that we are not dealing with this crisis alone. Every thing we do will and has direct affects on our families. If you think by not thinking or talking about your problems they are just going to disappear? You're absolutely wrong! They are not, going no where. What might disappear is your family; they might wind up getting tired of your nonsense and leave you. Your home might disappear if you don't budget your money right, your nice car might disappear if don't keep on the payment's and you will end up on the bus and with out a home! Most of all your sanity might disappear because you losing everything might leave you insane.

YOUR TWO OPTIONS

If you have become a victim of the recession depression what are you going to do now? Are you going to go see an expensive therapist? I don't think you are unless you got a good insurance plan that will cover that. I'm sure if your unemployed you don't even have healthcare no more. Thinking about joining some kind of help group that can offer you some kind of support during these hard times? Good luck finding one because if you do find a good therapist or support group they probably ran out of funding or don't have anymore openings. I'm not saying this to discourage you. I am telling you this because no one ever bothered to tell me these things while I was out there looking for help. The truth is you only got two options and one is not a good one but unfortunately it's the one that most people decide to take. You can either turn to drugs, alcohol or go into the denial stage abusing some kind of substance. It may not even be a substance it just may be a destructive behavioral pattern that you developed due to your lack of work and stress that builds up inside of you. Destructive behavior can also lead you down the wrong path and make you wind up in a dead end street. These alternatives are in no way going to give you any positive results at all? They will only get you more in debt. Yes you will forget your problems for a while but that's the key word here it's only for a while! Once the affects wear off, your problems will still be there.

If you're already down that path when your reading my book please go get some help. Programs that see that you're really sincere about getting help will try and work with you. If you don't have money or insurance, try to look for a program that will offer you free services. Turn to one of your family members, and let them know that you are having a drug problem. If you don't have any family members find someone to talk to about your drug problem. There are plenty of programs and people that if you really want to clean are willing to help you in your time of need. I'm not here to judge no one I just want every one to know that there is help out there and that you are not alone. I want you to know as you read this book that there are many people out there and myself that really do care about what you are going through. Or you can be at that stage in your life where you feel like know one is taking the time to hear you out. I know for certain there is one Person that cares for you deeply, that person is you. We can continue living our life's the way we are not caring about tomorrow. Because we lost our home, our relationship didn't work out; we lost all ties with our family members these are all good reasons to lose hope.

But let me give you some advice no problem, big or small will last forever. I know some of life's problems are painful and make you want to just quit but why quit? So you can be another static? Another someone that couldn't or just plain out wouldn't try? Be that some one that gave life another try that fought back and made it when no one else said you could. Be that some one that makes it in life gets that nice car, gets that pretty woman or handsome man and lives happily ever after. Be that some one that makes all the people turn their heads while you walk down the street. The way we should look at life is as follows, if you lost your wife because you didn't have a job. Don't just sit around and feel sorry for your self get up as hard as it may seem, make some kind of effort to get back on your feet. Wash your face, iron your clothes, eat something look in the mirror and say to yourself today is the first day of my new life. Go look for a job, update that resume, and bring back that go-getter spirit you once had. I guarantee you if she really was in love with you she will come back, and if she doesn't that's okay too. You now have your act together go out there and get yourself another mate. Do things you couldn't do before if you choose to not date for a while that's okay too. Look at life as a win, win situation you get your life together you get your wife and all the things you lost back. If she doesn't come back or come to a mutual agreement for the children then take it as you still restored your life. Which means you will be able to work something out so you can see your kids again. So you can buy that house, pull that new car out of the dealership, But most of all so you can be happy again.

We don't really stop and notice that living our lives in this destructive way can and will affect us in the long run. You may not be going out there on a rampage it maybe by neglecting a loved one ignoring a significant other while there in need. Not even bothering to listen to our once close friends? Lets not let this economy break us lets stay strong through these tuff times and do what's right don't worry about what others might think. That person you are ignoring might be on the verge of doing something drastic, or about to throw there life away to drugs, or do some other act of random foolishness they might later regret! Yes we live in a nation where greed controls some individual, yes our government isn't perfect, and yes we cannot change everyone. What we can do is change ourselves. A different you equals a different us and a different us equals a different them and with them you cant mess with!

WHY HOLD ON WHEN YOU HAVE RAN OUT OF REASONS

I will be the first to admit saying that you need someone to talk to is pretty hard to do. I spent many nights alone wondering if any one cared. I know as a man its hard to show your feelings due to the fact that we are scared that someone is going to judge us .The truth is everyday more people are doing more good than bad. Everyday you see places giving free food and offering a helping hand. Now they can't force you to get on your feet all they can do is lend you a hand so that you can pick yourself up. You must make the choice yourself"Is this going to be a new beginning for you or the end"? I understand that all of this seems like a nightmare that you can't get yourself out of. But once again it's just for a little while you will get through all of this and in the future you can explain it to others that you defeated the economy monster.

I know that we are here on this earth for a purpose from the everyday common person you see who sits behind a desk next to the top dog of the company.

Without the worker ants there is no colony because the largest numbers in the colony. Consist of the worker ants which in this example are you and I play the role of the worker ants. That do all the work and that carry all the heavy weight. Most of all in the colonies time of need we do whatever it takes to survive. Many people don't realize how important the worker ant's are. Yes some people are meant to be leaders and others are meant to be followers.

The truth of the matter is you can't make an army with out no soldiers. If you have never heard this before I'm here to tell you that with out you there is one less wheel on the car and like a car with only three wheels. It can be moved but it will not function and move the way it was intended. I feel everyone is needed to make this country the great country that it was intended to be.

We need all the stay home moms, and day care people who tend to our kids .Without them we could not even go to work .We need all the factories, warehouse workers, mail men, and woman and truckers as well .Without them who would manufacture store and deliver our products. Without these individuals that work at the post office we wouldn't be able to obtain our everyday items, and wouldn't be able to receive or send out mail. Receive those letters we have been waiting for or those packages we are expecting from over seas or just down the street. We need all those people that work in countless offices all over the United States .Customer services representatives, Secretaries, filing clerks, shipping and receiving personnel. Without these people there would be no where to process our documents or people to take are calls and assist us when we are in need. There would be no one to assure all shipments get from place to place. Law enforcement, the medical fields and fire fighters help to assure that we are in good care. Imagine a world where there was no law enforcements, medical personal or fire fighters? We would have no one to call for help in case of an emergency or if we got hurt. We would have no one to rescue us or our belongings from a disaster or life treating event. Regardless if it's a minor or major event that takes place in our community. These people are there when we need them. We need all the environment protection personnel that keep our planet as clean as possible of pollution and waste. So that our children will have that same chance to run and play and live as many years on it as we did. Our F.D.A personnel to inspect and make sure our food is properly made and packaged. We need all of our janitorial people to keep our public places, parks and schools clean. So that our children may attend classes there and use clean bathrooms and eat in clean cafeterias. Most of all we need all the people that teach in our classrooms all over the United States. They are the biggest piece to the puzzle we call life. Without them we would all be ignorant and uneducated and would not be able to get those degrees or credentials we are trying to get. Without a teacher we won't have the common knowledge to move forward. There is really no way to learn and achieve the things we need to know to get a good job or follow a certain career. That's why I say they play the most critical role in our lives and deserve more recognition for what they do. If we didn't have these people that taught us all the basic concepts we have learned in grade school I wouldn't even be writing this book today. When it was brought to my attention that teacher's only get paid once a month it broke my heart because they are the back bone to this world.

WHAT RESOURCES DO WE HAVE?
WHO CAN WE TURN TO?

When you're unemployed the resources that the government has to offer are slim to none. Their services are limited to how many people can attend and be helped that's a fact. We must take it upon ourselves to look for support in our families and if we don't have any, we must then turn to our closest friends. Being unemployed we must try to get involved in some kind of workshops or some kind of activity that will improve our skills. It may be going back to school for some, taking a computer class, or switching to a whole new trade for others. Along time ago I learned that everything has a beginning and an end. That theory can be applied to all aspects of life it may be a good one or a bad one. If we are going through a hard time we must remember that this is only temporary. That with the right tools and adequate resources we can turn any situation around for the better.

The one resource that I know is completely free and has no limits to seating is ones faith whatever it may be we must keep it strong. This is the time to turn to your beliefs may it be Buddha, Jesus Christ, Ala, or whatever kind of belief you may have. Whatever, whoever you may pray to. This is the time to reach out to them and ask for the strength you need to keep holding on. I'm not saying this is your only option I'm just making a suggestion. I am a strong believer that in a time of desperation and hopelessness man tends to turn to the super natural. It doesn't matter if you pray to an image, an idol, if it has one head or ten. Has no arms or has ten arms, if it's human or out of this world. Or even if you believe in Science you got to stick to what you believe in these hard times.

Now moving on to your job seeking skills and resources, when it comes to job hunting don't just rely on using the internet or the newspaper. Get out their and do some kind of foot work. Instead of purchasing food while you're looking for work get in the routine of making a lunch. Something that you can just carry around with you that won't get spoiled. Try going to job agencies, look for jobs in the penny saver, try cold calling in the yellow pages. Which means look up an area in the yellow pages that you use to work in and call them to see if they are hiring? Keep track of all the jobs you went to in a binder type of book. Stating what day and time you went. With the name of the person you gave your application to and a number to follow up on your application.

I will be honest with you; sometimes we just have to put our pride down and take a lower paying job, or even work a shift we really don't want to work. Just to get back on our feet and get ourselves going again.

Stay in the routine of waking up early so if you do get a job that requires you to do so you're not struggling to get use to it again. I know it's not easy and with so many people out there in competition. Applying and sending their resume to the same jobs you've applied for. It might seem like your chances of getting the job are slim to none.

That's not necessarily true! You have to make yourself stand out from the rest of the crowd. When I say stand out from the crowd I don't mean walk out of your interview tap dancing. I mean try wearing a tie and a nice button shirt for your interview maybe even some slacks. If you don't have any of the items I just mentioned and think that those items are too expensive for you to buy right now. You can go down to your neighborhood thrift store or goodwill and get them there for cheap.

Even getting a certificate in the area you're applying for will make you stand out in an interview. Going back to school for a higher accreditation like an associates or a bachelors degree always looks good on an interview and in your resume. Or you can just simply clean up your act while on an interview. Meaning be more polite, comb your hair and spray some of that fancy cologne if you have some. Not too much though we don't want them to have to evacuate the building with respirators and have to escort you out. Show up at least ten minutes early to show your punctuation skills. Practice on being more confident but not too cocky neither. Do a little research on the company that you are applying for before you go. An employer will always be impressed if you go in their already knowing a little something about the place you are applying for. Another good tip is making sure you wear dress shoes with laces. When on an interview if the employer sees you with slip-ons he will think you are lazy and you can't even take the time to tie your shoes. (You'll be surprise on what these employers think).

WHO WILL GET LAID OFF?

The chances of you getting laid off from your job are very high, and that's the honest to god truth. I'm not going to sit here and lie to you, we are all at risk as long as our economy is in the state that it's in. There is nothing you can do to make your employer get out of debt our make California's debt go away. If your company is going through hard times right now and are facing financial troubles. You are most likely to receive a pink slip and join the millions of people all across the nation that is unemployed. It's not about how good you deal with getting laid off? How well you take the bad news? Or whether or not you have a savings account to back you up? What really matters is how quick you bounce back on your feet, and how well you handle the pressure of being unemployed. Most important of all how do you plan on bouncing back? Becoming unemployed is something that is becoming more and more common. It's like catching the common cold; it's easy to catch, but hard to get rid of! We must be prepared physically, and mentally during these hard times we are in. I think the reason why times are harder in this day and age is because all the technology we have now. Back in the days there were no cell phones, or high tech automobiles. The point that I am trying to get across is now that we have these items we have to worry about more expensive bills like the car payment or not going over the minutes on our phones. We have to keep our faith strong and not let things overwhelm us we must stay clear minded and stayed focused. Not only for our sake but for the sake of our children whose happiness we are jeopardizing if we don't get our lives back on track.

WHY IS IT HARD TO RELY ON AID OR UNEMPLOYMENT?

The thing with unemployment and government aid is that there are so many people that are either trying to get it, or are already on it. You can't just walk in there and say "I need assistance" and it be delivered to you on a platter. You are practically in a race trying to beat your neighbor once you lose your job. If you have never gone to the welfare offices trust me you don't want to go. It's nothing nice you got to pull a number in a small room with all kinds of people that are also trying to apply for some kind of help. There's people there and all kinds of kids running around out of control and bouncing off the walls. While there mom is sit in a row of plastic chairs and talking on her cell phones. Don't get me wrong there are a lot of people, who really need to receive some help and get medical attention. But some people just go too far with the whole welfare thing they start doing all kinds of fraudulent things like claiming kids that don't exist. Getting unemployment and working under the table. Getting unemployment or have child care for their kids while they suppose ably go to school. But they don't even bother to go; they take advantage of the whole education thing. If you really need help with your finances, health, or child care you should be sincere and honest about it and not try to get over on the system. Because in the end the only one that pays the consequence is you! Even being on aid is not a privilege or something to be proud of. The whole purpose of it is so you can get back on your feet and get off of aid. It was not made for you to stay on it and get your toes done, and buy your lazy boyfriend clothes or your kid a video game. So you can keep them busy and out of your hair while you have company come over and party at night. I m not trying to criticize anyone I just believe that we should not take advantage of what little government funded programs we do have. Hundreds of people are relying on unemployment and aid not knowing that these things can get cut at anytime. If these things were to be cut tomorrow we would honestly be in worst conditions than what we are in now.

It's never too late...

With all sorts of life's problems I have dealt,

Many mixed emotions I have felt.

`Living my life the best I could

In the past not always making the best choices I should.

Thinking there was no way out feeling stressed out made me want to scream out of anger and shout.

Regretting the day I was born,

From my book of my life the chapter of hope was torn.

Assuming in my narrow mind there was no way out

Thinking and acting like a child at the time I would pout.

After years of struggles and pain,

When all was said and done I thanked god for the knowledge I gained.

Realizing my life was not over,

No more turning to drugs or alcohol or any type of destructive behavior. I am able to deal with life with a clear mind and sober.

So as a person that once sat in the same chair you did, as an unemployed individual and a troubled child. Who was uneducated and uninformed through the garden of ignorance I ran wild?

Not long ago when I was a kid.

Just like most people do and did...

Getting educated will be the birth of a new you equipped with all the tools; you need to deal with life's stress and strife.

And remember that getting an education is a good step that any person could take in their life..........

Written and felt by *Victor Zapata* 1/20/09

WHY CUT SCHOOL FUNDING AND LAY OFF TEACHERS?

There are a lot of teachers and school programs that are getting cut due to the economy. Which I feel is nonsense. I believe the government should have looked at cutting school funding as the last resort not part of the top twelve! What is going to happen when our kids go to school the next day and there teacher is no longer there. Yes you can replace the teacher. But you can't replace the bond that a student has developed with his or her teacher. If you really sit down and do the math. Let's say a student is in a class room with a teacher for at least 6 hours a day. This equals 30hours a week and equals 120 hours a month, 6,240 hours a year! I would think that a child would become very close to his or her teacher after spending that many hours together. Yet regardless of all these facts the government still wants to cut school funding. From what I hear they even want to cut physical education now. Why would we want to do that? When our kids are becoming more and more obese every year? If we cut out the physical education part of our kids lives they will become more obese. From lack of exercise and will lose all interest in staying physically fit. Honestly what are parents suppose to do if that happens? The average parent doesn't educate themselves on obesity. So how is he or she going to without any training or proper information educate their kids. Many of them hardly even see their kids due to the fact that they are working two jobs to support their families. So who will educate our children? (Now that is a million dollar question).

They want to cut the art classes in schools which I think is truly sad. That's like telling a kid he or she can't be creative or use there imagination. Art is a very important class that allows one to not only express them selves in a creative manner. It gives them the chance to learn about past artist and how art has change through out the ages. How it is connected to a gallery, a mural, or a sketch composite drawn to find a criminal.

Many people look at classes like music and art as unnecessary. Close your eyes and imagine a world without art and music. This place would have no certain series of colors or shape to catch your eye. There would be no symphonies that would soothe your ear and make you sway your body uncontrollably. No images of the past to make your mind wonder about that certain period of time and make you smile. This place that we would find ourselves in with no visual beauty or sound would be a terrible place to live in.

That is why I feel if there are no art classes or music programs available for our kids to express themselves in, how are they going to do it? Are they going to start acting out in school? Join the wrong crowd? Start using drugs turn to violence due to the lack of being able to express them selves. I just don't feel its right that we deny the kids of this day and age to have fun, be creative, like past generations have done. To take advantage of the many great programs you and I have had a chance to attend.

Our educational system might have not been the best, but it sure has trained many qualified and successful individuals. That helps us on a daily basis from; Doctors, to Teachers, Police Officers, Firemen, and Nurses.

WHAT WILL OUR KIDS OR ADULTS DO WITH NO AFTER SCHOOL PROGRAMS OR VOCATIONAL OPENINGS AVAILABLE?

I don't want to think about what will become of our kids if a lot of our schools funding gets cut. I don't see any logical reason to do what the state of California is doing. I think the people in Sacramento are making a huge mistake by passing this proposed bill. They need to really sit down and look at the big picture. Let's say they cut a day out of the week for our kids not to go to school. Do they really realize what kind of impact that will have on a person's life that uses school as day care? What I mean by that is that on a typical day that certain parent drops his or her child off at school and then heads to work after. By the government cutting that certain child's school day you now have broken the cycle that the parent had developed to go to work. Which means that parent will now either have to miss work to sign her child up for daycare which might cost her job. Due to the long waiting period that is required to apply for childcare. Resulting in that parent losing his or her job because missing work right now is not a bright idea. Which may cause them to get backed up on their bills, and not afford there rent and wind up on aid. What is this government trying to do make the number of people on aid and unemployment higher? Well that's exactly what they are doing by making this type off cut to our school funding and government programs. They don't realize that these types of actions will not only affect the parents of kids in school. Teacher's that teach our children will be affected, along with the bus drivers that drive our kids to school. The crossing guard that crosses your child across the street in the morning will also be affected. Everyone on aid or unemployment will be affected by these issues also. The large number of people on these programs might make the government start to cut back on their funding. The higher the numbers are of people that are unemployed, make it difficult for you to get a job.

Let's say the parent doesn't qualify for state child care for whatever the reason maybe. He or she will now be forced to pay someone out of their own pocket to watch his or her children. Either they will have to pay more money or make good judgment on watching them their selves. As a person who has paid for child care depending of what kind of care you are looking for and how many kids you have it might seem like a car payment!

You can look for a state facility but that's expensive and they only can watch so many kids at a time.

Oftentimes the parent is forced to settle for a cheaper alternative that might end up being a more dangerous one. In everyday life kids are getting kidnapped, and people getting robbed at gun point are becoming common. So why would we want our kids to be out of school early or not at school at all? And jeopardize there safety or even there lives? The truth is I would rather have my child at school or in day care where he or she is safe.

Cutting back on school funding will make a huge impact on people of every age I think. For example a grown up whom for whatever reason didn't take advantage of the opportunity they had to get their diploma in the past. They will no longer have the opportunity to attend adult school. Some people don't get the second chance at getting his or her diploma. But even getting the basic knowledge a person needs to know feels good and can be helpful in the future. Adult education is a way for a person to go back and prove to the world that they deserve a second chance. Getting a diploma will not only build individuals self esteem but it may make them want to higher their education.

Adult school offers several programs that I believe are necessary for people of our community. Such programs as the many occupational training programs they have. Their computer classes and the G.E.D classes also are helpful to the community needs. What message are we trying to send to the young people and grown adults of our communities? By no longer offering the classes they need to become more productive members of society. Are we going to send them a message that becoming educated is not important in life? In a good case scenario that child will learn what he needs to know to get by in life on its own. In a worst case scenario if we deny that child there right to get a complete education. That child will soon grow up not having any interest in school or have a bad perspective of our school system. When he or she has a child or children, they will pass the seed of ignorance to there children. Before you know it, cities will be filled with chaos, ignorant and negative people. With no interest in school or changing the way they think and look at schooling. Those cities may turn into states and those states may turn into our country. Then how will we contain something that we have planted and started? How do you unsay a spoken word? How do you undo an act which has already been committed? You can't!

My life story

M any of the things that were written in this book came directly out of the pages of my life. With that in mind let me give you a little insight on my actual life story. My name is Victor Eduardo Zapata, and I'm 25 years old. I worked in a company for three years whose name I would rather not mention. Do to legal action that is being taken against them at this present time and date. I use to love my job I loved it so much, that I became a work alcoholic and would rather be at work than at home. I know it's sad to say but I got hooked on working and making money which was my first mistake. My second mistake happened when I gave my company my cell phone number.

Because this meant they had access to me 24 hours a day, seven days a week. I was the first person they contacted when things went wrong. When something was missing, when the machine was broken I mean it felt like they had me on their speed dial. My next mistake was that I let my problems at work get tangled up with my problems at home which turned into a bigger problem. Problems at home and problems at work are the perfect ingredients for a bowl of disaster. Whenever these two ingredients are combined no matter in what sequence regardless of the amounts they still equal disaster. There was no escaping this harsh reality, I had mixed this big mess and now I had to take a big sip of it.

I put up with all the nonsense at my job and stood there as long as I did due to the fact that I had a family to worry about. I had four kids to worry about at home and I didn't want them to go without. If I would have decided to quit my job I had to make sure that I had a job lined up right after quitting. Unlike someone with no kids who just can quit their job without having a second thought. I had a lot of bills to pay every month rent, utilities, and accessories. I really don't know how I pulled it off; I must have been blessed with special powers.

Dealing with drama at home and at work wasn't easy on me. It was a miracle I didn't wind up in an asylum. Things at work started to get really bad they started to short me on my checks and began to force me to work more hours than I could handle. I was already dying I guess this was the grand finale. I was being verbally abused at work by my supervisor and human resources were not helping me at all. I remember the first time I went to the H.R. dept. I was so nervous and they made me feel so comfortable. When approaching the H.R department they told me that they would handle the situation for me. That was all a bunch of lies because minutes later my supervisor went down there and personally escorted me back to my work station. Not before he threw in his two cents about how I had abandoned my work station. This company was straight up corrupted and they didn't care about there workers at all. All they cared about was production they were like hungry dogs fighting over a bone. The more we gave them the more they wanted. I never got no holidays off I worked regular time, over time, double time; it all seemed to me like I was doing hard time. The supervisors were in cahoots with each other it felt like they had some kind of secret organization going on. It felt like if one of the supervisors yelled at me for something, before my shift was over I was hearing it from someone else.

The funny part of it all was that they fired me for some bogus reason. I thought that since I had filed for unemployment I qualified without a doubt. Then I could get unemployment and I could go look for a better job because that job was just not worth it. I did the right thing when I went to the human resources department and reported all the incidents that had taken place and they fired me anyways. I wanted to be a hero and stand up for all the workers that were getting abused, mistreated, short handed on there checks. There were rumors going around that the supervisors were saying that my work performance was shitty. I decided to let it go and keep my dignity (so I walked away).

I was going to do things the right way, file for unemployment and take legal action against them in court. Well things didn't go the way I had imagined them to go I applied for unemployment then a few weeks later got denied. I appealed it! Only to go to a board meeting which was not in my favor? The commissioner had no clue what was going on with both parties. We were being recorded and I said my side of the story and they said there's. What I thought was more ridicules was that my supervisor cried a couple of fake tears and said that he had always been there for me when I needed him. That his heart went out to me and my new born son? My new born son I took into thought how pathetic he sounded I had a new born little girl. He knew that I had a girl not a boy, because he has seen her countless of times. I took check stubs, and a letter of recognition written by the C.E.O of the company and still got denied. When I received the second letter informing me that I was denied my unemployment once again by my employer I was furious. I mean what kind of world do we live in when the corporate monster can get a way with that kind of nonsense? It said why would he go in there and lie? Common sense buddy his job was on the line I bet! I m sure that the company or his boss told him that I better not win that case or he would be fired. I appealed it for a third time, but this time to the court of appeals and still got denied again. I felt like I had honestly just got raped? I needed that money and they denied me my unemployment because I couldn't take the abuse and nonsense no more! What upset me the most was that I worked for that money and felt that I was entitled to it?

I looked for work every where and went through agencies but with the economy going bad I was looking and looking but not finding anything. Things got really hard for my girlfriend and I, we struggled a lot. We went through her school loan money, my 401k and all our savings in a matter of months. I got a couple temporary jobs here and there but it wasn't cutting it. My family and I were forced to move out of our home and go live at my girlfriend's mom's house. Which was nothing nice just picture six people living in one room it was super crowded. We had nowhere to store our personal belongings so we rented two storages.

I was working temporarily for an agency, and my girlfriend was working as well. I thought things were going to get better with us, well they didn't? My girlfriend was getting food stamps to help us out with the food part at least. Well it cost her, her job because they always wanted to see her at odd times and she worked in west L.A. She had to keep explaining things to her boss. Her boss explained to her that they were unable to keep a person that wasn't going to stay the whole shift. She got fired from her job I got laid off from mine and that's were the nightmare began. Now we had no choice but to go file for assistance and cash aid so we did. It was horrible we sat there all day and when we did get seen the lady couldn't even remember my girlfriend name. She kept confusing her with her mom. You can already guess what happened then, they put my girlfriend's case together with her mom's case. "The mess is unexplainable". They always sent my girlfriend termination letters, and notices that they were going to cancel her childcare. Our child care provider was always getting paid late or not at all. I'm being serious there was one month were they didn't pay the lady for 5 months and she was fed up already.

From this point things only got worse for us we didn't have a place to stay so we ended up homeless and living in a hotel room with all of our kids. You can imagine what it was like. We were all cramped up in this little hotel room try to compromise on where we all going to sleep. We had no stove at all and could only eat microwaveable things.We lived in a hotel for like three months and things got worse they were going to cut my girlfriends childcare. If I didn't get a job so I had to get of her case and move out of her house. I did it for my kids I didn't want my kids to not have child care and end up with no where to stay.

When I moved I didn't have nowhere to go, so I went to homeless shelters and hit the food banks to get something to eat. I would shower wherever I could and carry a little case of all my hygiene items. That I would use everyday things like; my tooth brush, my deodorant, soap whatever fit in my pockets. All my clothes I bought from the thrift store or the good will that was all I could afford so I just did without. I had one pair of interview clothes a black shirt and some brown slacks. I tried my hardest not to get it dirty because I couldn't afford to wash them. My relatives were embarrassed of me and didn't want anything to do with me. They had there own financial problems to deal with and they weren't going to babysit me while I was down in the gutter.

I lived like this for 8 months until finally I got my tax form and was able to do my taxes. I got myself a room to stay in and helped out my family with the little things they needed help with. I told myself that I was not going to lose hope and I haven't. I honestly believe that I went through all these hard times to appreciate things more. I had a family and I ignored them, I had a job and even though it wasn't the best of jobs I took it for granted. I had a beautiful girlfriend at home and I couldn't tell her how I felt. I was to prideful and I didn't want to be humbled by no one well being homeless is the best thing to humble a person! A year late I 'm still struggling to keep a steady job, my girlfriend an I still aren't on the best of terms. We still have our occasional arguments here and there. I know that there is light at the end of the tunnel, even though I have came to a cross road in my life. At the moment I might not know which way to turn or where to go. I know as long as I have my family and have a positive attitude nothing will overwhelm me. When something big comes crashing down, I now know how to remove myself from these circumstances. Whatever road I decide to take it will be the right one, the road to happiness?

BE CAREFUL WHOSE ADVICE YOU TAKE

Many people take advice from expensive counselors and shrinks, buying expensive books written by people that have never been broke. Have never been affected by the economy or are going through hard times. Why me? It's simple because I was broke, I lost my home, I became homeless and my fiancé left me because I couldn't get a job. I ended up on the streets on drugs and was having thoughts of suicide. I know what it feels like when you can't see your kids because you're fighting with your mate. I have been in huge debt before with my credit cards. My mortgage plan went bad due to the banks running out of money. I lived in a hotel because I had no where else to go. I have felt so stressed out that my vision has gone blurred. I have been up all night crying to myself wishing that I wasn't born. I was ignored by my own family; I have had the door slammed in my face by many jobs due to the economy. I know what it's like when you apply at all kinds of places just to get the run around. I've sat at agencies for hours hopping that they might get me a job and they don't. I've been on their famous list, I have gotten ignored and have been told yeah, yeah your on the list will give you a call and they don't even get your information down. When in reality they didn't write your name or number. Trust me I know what it's like to ride the bus looking for work because my car got repossessed. I have been forced to claim bankruptcy because I was way over my head in debt. I have felt too embarrassed to ask for help from anyone. I have wasted 30 minutes of my time on the phone with calling the unemployment office just to get hung up on by some damn automated voice system.

I really care about what you're going through because I actually went through it. I have hit rock bottom in my life. I've been at a crossroad and didn't know which way to go next. These are some of the reasons why I can tell you how it feels. I have been broke without a dollar to my name, and wondered what my family is going to eat to night? Or were we going to sleep tomorrow? My fridge has been empty; I have gone to food banks to get food for my kids to eat. I have shopped at thrift stores, and the good will. I have panhandled just to get a bite to eat, as embarrassing as that sounds I have done it. I have lived in homeless shelters, I have been incarcerated, and I have been on drugs.

All the experience I have I learned hands on in the school of hard knocks. Not because I read some book at the library or at night school. I didn't take a course at a secondary school and decide to become an economical crisis counselor, Not that there is something wrong with that. I just believe that everything is expressed in a deeper way, when it's your stomach that's growling because you haven't eaten all day. When it's your wallet that's empty and when your stuck without a job.

Sometimes people want to hear it from someone that has experienced what they have gone through. I hope this book opens your eyes as a person that is unemployed and as a person that is employed also. You never know if you might be next and sometimes the suspense of not knowing if it's going to be you is worse than getting laid off .

THE RECESSION DEPRESSION

I got the recession depression, and I feel the aggression building up inside me...

Sitting in my car stressed out, and mad in my mind, rehearsing a good story or ways to tell my family we just lost the only source of incoming we had!

How could this be? Turning to god and asking why this is happening to me???

Had I not suffered enough, what else could I possibly go through???

I waited and waited and realized so many people are praying to god in heaven my prayer might not have gone through...

How could I go home and face my loving, caring, and understanding fiancé of five years that the ring she picked out has to go back...

The strength to tell her I truly lack...

Picturing her beautiful brown eyes filled with tears bringing to life my worst fears as I imagine her heart in two pieces slowly cracked...

Sitting in my car trying to ignore the voices screaming inside...

Fighting back the tears that build up in my eyes, refusing to show emotion because I got far too much pride...

I need to think of a plan, my savings and that's when it hit me I don't have one and emergency savings I have none...

What should I do! My life is through!

How are we going to get by? The thought of this whole mess makes me want to break down and cry...

Tears dripping down my face, eyes tightly shut deep bags under my eyes from my body being so sleep deprived and tired...

My body drained, exhausted, my mind replaying over and over earlier in the day when I got fired...

My boss saying I feel for you I really do?? But what can I do?? Trying his hardest to sound sad, I'm just a worker like you it's the economy that's doing bad...

I got the Recession Depression

Claiming at that very moment insanity...I turn to profanity...

Out of my car now yelling at the top of my lungs
yet to the people walking on the side walks I
am invisible for their hearts remorse lack...

Yes I lost control and bad habits claimed my soul

*I now realize that all the mistakes I made in the
past will slowly but surely on me take a toll.*

*Even though all that time I lost, and the price of
happiness to me came at the highest cost*

*I'm glad I went though all those tuff times that
made me stumble along the way*

*Because all the falls I experienced made me who
I am today...*

Written and felt by Victor Zapata.

www.ingramcontent.com/pod-product-compliance
Lightning Source LLC
Chambersburg PA
CBHW021238280526
45784CB00005B/2138